nice girl's book of
naughty spells

Get rich, Get lucky, Get even

DEBORAH GRAY

Journey Editions
Tokyo • Rutland, Vermont • Singapore

Published by Journey Editions, an imprint of Periplus Editions (HK) Ltd., with editorial offices at 364 Innovation Drive, North Clarendon, Vermont 05759 U.S.A., by arrangement with HarperCollins*Publishers*, Sydney.

First published in 1998 by HarperCollins*Publishers* Pty Limited, Australia as *The Mini Book of Magic Spells*.

Library of Congress Catalog Card Number: 99–62469

ISBN-10: 1–885203–88–8
ISBN-13: 978-1-885203-88-5

Distributed by

North America, Latin America & Europe
Tuttle Publishing
364 Innovation Drive
North Clarendon, VT 05759-9436 U.S.A.
Tel: 1 (802) 773-8930
Fax: 1 (802) 773-6993
info@tuttlepublishing.com
www.tuttlepublishing.co

Asia Pacific
Berkeley Books Pte. Ltd.
61 Tai Seng Avenue #02-12
Singapore 534167
Tel: (65) 6280-1330
Fax: (65) 6280-6290
inquiries@periplus.com.sg
www.periplus.com

First edition

10 09 08 07   10 9 8 7

Cover and internal illustrations by Sue Ninham

Printed in Singapore

TUTTLE PUBLISHING® is a registered trademark of Tuttle Publishing, a division of Periplus Editions (HK) Ltd.

DEBORAH GRAY

Australia's Good Witch was born into a long heritage of Celtic magick and mysticism. Initiated as a teenager into an Ancient Druid Circle, she has studied parapsychology and alchemy for over twenty years and inherited her knowledge of metaphysics from one of the world's few remaining Druid Masters. In addition to writing a highly successful weekly column for *New Idea* magazine, Deborah holds lectures and workshops in metaphysics and spellcasting. She is the co-author of the international bestseller, *How to Turn your Ex-Boyfriend into a Toad*, and, following the Bardic tradition of inspirational music and verse, she is also an award-winning songwriter.

To contact Deborah regarding her catalogue
and lectures, write to:
PO Box 229, Woollahra NSW 2025 Australia
website: www.deborahgraymagic.com
email: witchg@mpx.com.au

CONTENTS

☆

Magic is real and wishes can come true!

✯ Casting a spell is a beautiful and inspiring ritual that connects us to the endless power within the natural world and ourselves. I truly believe that our lives can be filled with miracles and abundance when we open our souls to the enchanted universe around us.

As every fun-loving witch knows, we could all do with a dash of extra passion and prosperity in our hectic lives. Goddess Power and Magick are not only about pretty angels and fairy wings. Just like the universal strength of Mother Nature, we can also connect with the 'Warrior Queen' – strong, protective and assertive, as well as the soft and nurturing 'Bright Maiden'.

And yes, sometimes even nice girls need a little 'Sorcery for Stress' to help ward off the occasional busybody or frog prince.

Of course, there's no real mischief intended or harm done towards anyone. It's all about rebuilding your self-esteem, opening yourself up to love and success, and completely letting go of any resentment and bitterness. The results are absolutely amazing! You'll be back to your perky self in no time, bringing closure to old worries, glowing with positive newfound energy and ready to magically take on the world!

> 'WITH THE WAVE OF A WAND
> AND A DASH OF SCENTED SPICE
> AND FLOWER,
> OUR SPIRITS ARE LIFTED
> AND DREAMS WILL COME TRUE;
> THIS IS THE MAGICK HOUR.'

☆

Deborah Gray

Love Spells

PASSION POWER

I'm a luvv planet

☆ The funny thing about Magic is that the more you become centred in your own universe, the more others will want to visit your world. This spell is a great preparation to help loved ones spin back into your orbit.

During a quiet moment, light some vanilla incense and close your eyes for a few minutes while you breathe calmly and rid yourself of nervous thoughts and desires. Then repeat these magic words:

☆

'I AM CONTENT IN MY OWN UNIVERSE, I CREATE AND GIVE LOVE AND FRIENDSHIP AND I WILL GROW AND LEARN TO KNOW MY INNER SELF.'

Attracting a soul mate

YOU WILL NEED TO GATHER:

- *clean white clothing*
- *sandalwood incense*
- *a red candle*

☆ The best time to perform this spell is on the night of a full moon.

Yes, I know. We're all tempted to ask for 'tall dark and handsome' or 'stunning and sexy', but tsk! tsk! Isn't it more important to really think about which type of personality and inner being would enhance and complement your life? Well, once you've pondered on that one for a while, take a shower and then get dressed in some clean white clothing.

Next, light the incense and the candle and sit quietly nearby while you relax your body and focus your mind on the type of person you would like to attract, and repeat this incantation:

'WITH THE SPIRIT OF AVALON,
THROUGH THE WISDOM OF MERLIN,
I OPEN MY MIND AND HEART TO
RECEIVE TRUE LOVE.'

Bring back my love

YOU WILL NEED TO GATHER:

- *orange essence*
- *a photograph or drawing of your ex-love*
- *a mirror*

⭐ On a Friday night at 8 pm, light some orange essence and hold the image of your ex-love in your hand as you concentrate on seeing the two of you together again. Feel confident and happy as you repeat this magic quatrain:

Seal the spell's power by sticking the photograph or drawing of your ex-love face down against your bedroom mirror. Each time you pass by, send your ex a loving thought.

'TO SEE YOUR EYES AGAIN, MY LOVE, TO GAZE AT MY OWN REFLECTION ⭐ THERE, TO WALK SIDE BY SIDE IN STEP WITH YOU. SO SHALL MY REQUEST BE HEARD.'

Spice up your love

✰ Ever wondered how the Spice Girls were so effective at seducing the world with their sexy moves and music? Well, spices can help weave a powerful spell, and whether you are a blonde, brunette or redhead their vibrations will hot up your looks and lust power. Choose which spice is right for you then sprinkle it around you clockwise in a circle as you say:

IF YOU ARE BLONDE
*choose Cinnamon spice
for extra charisma.*

IF YOUR HAIR
IS BROWN
*use Nutmeg as your
spice, and a wealthy
lover is sure to look
your way.*

EBONY TRESSES
*will shine with
glamour from the
aromatic power of
Basil.*

THE SASSY REDHEAD
*can do no wrong if she
fires up her chances
with a charm made
from Ginger – or, if
she dares, a dash of
Paprika.*

'MAGIC CHARMS OF HERB AND SPICE,
NOW BECKON MY LOVED ONE
.............................★ TOWARDS ME IN A TRICE!'

Come to me

YOU WILL NEED TO GATHER:

- *a slim pink candle*
- *a clean carpenter's nail*
- *jasmine essence*
- *the green thorn of a red rose*

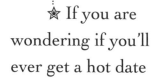

☆ If you are wondering if you'll ever get a hot date with you know who, now is your chance to send out all the right 'come hither' signals.

With the nail, engrave the initials of your intended into the side of the candle and then, with your index finger, anoint it from top to bottom with a little of the jasmine essence. Place the candle near a window so the moonlight can shine onto it. Then light it and watch the candle until it melts down completely. When the wax has cooled, squeeze some juice from the rose thorn over the top while you say:

'WITHER YOU GO,
YOUR HEART DOES KNOW.
I AM OF THE ROSE
AND THE ONE FOR YOU.'

I do I do

☆ You have found your Mr Right but he's being a bit slow with the marriage proposal. Cast this spell on Friday, the day of Venus, and you'll be choosing that diamond ring in no time!

YOU WILL NEED TO GATHER:

● *a length of pink ribbon*

● *pink lipstick*

Take a luxurious bath
or shower and after
you have patted
yourself dry, stand
sky clad (the witches'
term for naked) in front
of the bathroom mirror
as you wrap a long
piece of pink ribbon
around your waist.
Write your boyfriend's
name on the mirror
with a pink lipstick

and then hold the loose
end of the ribbon in
your hands and imagine
that you are pulling
your lover towards you
as you repeat this
incantation:

Finish by taking off
the ribbon and keeping
it in a drawer in your
bedroom dresser.

'RIBBON OF LOVE, PULL HIM CLOSER,
RIBBON OF LOVE, TIE HIM TO ME.'

Like chocolate for chocolate

YOU WILL NEED TO GATHER:

- *red flowers*
- *two red candles*
- *gardenia essence*
- *chocolate ice cream*
- *dark chocolate flakes*
- *passionfruit pulp*
- *crème de menthe*

☆ One of the sweetest ways to hot up your sex life is with an erotic banquet of 'just desserts'. Along with your favourite aphrodisiac foods, you might like to include this recipe for passion.

Set your dinner table with red flowers and two red candles which have been anointed with a little essence of gardenia. Mix together in a chilled bowl some chocolate ice cream with flakes of dark chocolate and passion-fruit pulp. As you pour in a few drops of crème-de-menthe, repeat these magic words:

☆

'BY THE CARESS OF ADONIS AND GOLDEN APHRODITE, SO AWAKENS THE PASSION OF DESIRE.'

You're the one that I want

YOU WILL NEED
TO GATHER:

- *two cinnamon sticks*
- *purple thread and white thread*

- *a piece of chamois or suede leather*
- *a darning needle*
- *a wooden box*

☆ You've just seen your dream lover and there's no time to wait!

Tie the two cinnamon sticks together with purple thread and then wrap the sticks up tightly in the piece of chamois. Sew up the sides with white thread and repeat this incantation:

Put the leather pouch inside a wooden box and keep the box in a private place.

☆
'TIGHTLY, TIGHTLY WRAPS MY LOVE, QUICKLY, QUICKLY, HE IS THE ONE.'

Lover, where are you?

YOU WILL NEED
TO GATHER:

● *peppermint incense*

● *a piece of licorice*

● *a bowl of water*

☆ For every soul there is a companion who reflects our desire for love and commitment. To help steer you

26

in the right direction,
cast this spell on the
night of a new moon.

Place all your items of
enchantment onto a
table and light the
incense. Breathe calmly
for a few moments,
then put the licorice into
the bowl, gaze into

the water's reflection
and repeat this
incantation: ························

Keep the bowl near
your bed and your
dreams will send you
an important sign.

'WATER WATER, CLEAR MY VISION. ☆
IN THIS WORLD
LIVES MY OTHER HALF;
SHOW ME, O EROS, ON WHICH PATH
I SHOULD FIND HIM AT LAST.'

Desperate and dateless

YOU WILL NEED
TO GATHER:

- *a white cloth*
- *a pink candle*
- *pen and paper*

☆ Don't just sit there waiting by the telephone! Weave a little magic instead.

Cleanse your telephone by wiping down the receiver with a damp white cloth. Light a pink candle and calmly think about your intended lover. Write down his name eight times on a piece of pink paper and hold it while you repeat this incantation:

Wrap the paper up in a ball and leave it near your telephone for one month.

'GODDESS SALINA, HEAR MY PLEA, SEND MY LOVER'S WORDS TO ME.'

See me, feel me

YOU WILL NEED
TO GATHER:

- *white carnations*
- *a vase*
- *a photograph of your partner*
- *a pair of eyeglasses*

☆ Want to make sure your lover only has eyes for you?

During a full moon, make a small love altar in your bedroom by placing a vase of white carnations and a photograph of your partner on a table. Hold a pair of eyeglasses in your hand while you think about your partner and repeat this incantation:

Hold the glasses up to your eyes for a moment or two and imagine that you see a ray of light shining from them to your lover.

'OH SIRAJ, GLIMMER WITH LIGHT
TO REVEAL THE VISION OF LOVE.'

Enchanted wedding

✩ The ancient Druids celebrated the union of the Moon Goddess and the Sun God, and also the crowning of the May Queen and King. If you want to hold a truly enchanted wedding then why not incorporate some of these ancient marriage rites into your ceremony to bring luck and everlasting love?

The best location would be in a pretty garden or park and the most fortunate time is during a new or waxing moon.

Gather your friends and family around you in a tree-filled park or a garden. Create a heavenly fragrant scene by decorating with garlands of perfumed flowers, like jasmine, lily of the valley and honeysuckle. The bride and groom should wear white and both carry sheaves of wheat and rosemary to represent fertility and prosperity. After speaking your vows, place a wooden stick on the ground. As you both step over it, say these words:

'BY MYSTICAL MOON AND LIFE-GIVING SUN, WE HANDFAST OUR LOVE IN BLESSED UNION AS ONE.'

Shy guy

YOU WILL NEED
TO GATHER:

- *half a cup of sesame oil*
- *a few coriander leaves*
- *a glass bowl*
- *musk incense*
- *pencil and paper*

☆ If you're feeling too shy to make the first move, cast this spell during the first hour of morning sunlight.

Mix together in a glass
bowl the sesame oil
and coriander leaves.
Light the musk incense
and think about your
intended lover while
you repeat this
incantation: ⋯⋯⋯⋯⋯⋯⋯⋯⋯ ☆

Next, draw a stick
figure onto a piece of
paper. Dip your finger
into the sesame oil and
coriander mixture and
touch the drawing
while you repeat the
incantation three times.

'WHEN YOU FEEL
THIS TOUCH
YOU WILL
LOVE ME
SO MUCH,
WE WILL
BE TOGETHER
SOON.'

Keep the drawing in
your dresser drawer.

Perfect pair

YOU WILL NEED
TO GATHER:

- *a cup of mineral water*
- *a teaspoon of puréed pear*
- *a bowl and a silver teaspoon*

☆ Perfect your chances for attraction by casting this spell every day for seven days before you make your move.

Start on a Wednesday evening by mixing a potion consisting of a cup of mineral water and a teaspoon of puréed pear. Hold the teaspoon in your right hand and stir slowly and steadily while you repeat this incantation:

Then dip your index finger into the cup and wipe a little of the mixture over your lips. By the seventh day your words should be irresistible.

'ARIADNE, WEAVE YOUR THREAD OF LOVE AND EMOTION, GRANT ME MAGIC IN THIS POTION.'

Casanova

YOU WILL NEED
TO GATHER:

- *two hairs of a dog*
- *half a glass of white wine*
- *a wooden bowl and spoon*
- *a purple candle*
- *a flowerpot*

☆ 'Don't worry, honey, I'm just working late at the office.' Well, just to make sure, cast this spell on the night of a full moon.

Mix together in a wooden bowl two dog hairs and half a glass of white wine. Light a purple candle and breathe evenly for a few moments, releasing your mind and body of stress as you repeat this incantation:

Pour the mixture into a flowerpot and keep the pot near your front door.

'WITH THE HAIR OF DOG,
FROM THE FRUIT ON THE VINE, ☆
YOU'LL STOP YOUR WANDERING
AND STAY ALL MINE.'

How to dump him

YOU WILL NEED
TO GATHER:

- *blue paper and a pen*
- *a pebble*
- *a length of white wool*
- *two white candles*

✫ You had the best intentions, but it just didn't work out. How do you soften the blow of breaking up?

At midday on a Saturday, write your lover's name three times on a piece of blue paper. Wrap it around a small pebble and tie some white wool around the pebble until the paper is completely covered, leaving enough wool to tie a bow. Place the wrapped pebble between two lit white candles and repeat this incantation:

Then slowly unwrap the wool and think positive thoughts as you imagine your lover smiling as he moves away from you with no regrets.

'O BITTERSWEET LOVE,
I SET YOU FREE
ON THE WINGS OF THE DOVE.'

Beauty and Happiness

GODDESS CHARMS

Glamour spell

YOU WILL NEED TO GATHER:

- *geranium and lavender essences*
- *candles*
- *lavender talcum powder*

✯ Glamour goddesses aren't only found in Hollywood. In fact, the word 'glamour' comes from the following ancient enchantment, which will help you get that film star appeal.

Take an aromatherapy bath or shower using geranium and lavender essences and fill your bathroom with candles. Spend time luxuriating in the warm water. After you have dried yourself with a fluffy towel, sprinkle lavender talcum powder over your body as you say:

'I AM WOMAN, GODDESS OF BEAUTY AND LIFE, AS TATIANA AND ISIS BEFORE ME. I CHERISH AND ADORE MY MIND, SPIRIT AND BODY.'

Repeat this incantation whenever you feel tempted to hoe into that junk food!

Baby love

YOU WILL NEED TO GATHER:

- *apple-scented body cream*
- *a string of pearls (fake ones are fine)*

☆ For those who yearn to hear the patter of tiny feet, remember that fertility spells follow the female lunar month, so calculate when you ovulate and perform this 'Lunar Goddess' spell at that time.

Take a romantic shower (preferably with your partner) and then gently massage the apple-scented body cream into your skin, taking extra care around your tummy. Imagine that you and your partner's hands are glowing with a warm golden light which is filling all this area with life and warmth. Visualise that you are pregnant as you gently place the pearls around your neck and repeat these magic words:

'PRECIOUS JEWELS OF LUNAR,
I OFFER THIS ADORNMENT
IN HONOUR OF YOUR POWER.
LET FERTILE LIGHT SHINE
THROUGH ME. O BLESSED BE.'

Secret oasis

☆ To help you deal with those daily pressures, make a time for yourself where you can perform this calming ritual. Sit down and close your eyes for a few minutes while you breathe deeply, relaxing your mind and body. In your mind's eye, imagine that you are surrounded by a lush green forest that is full of singing birds and sunshine.

A beautiful lady walks towards you and as she softly takes your hand she says:

☆

'WELCOME TO YOUR OASIS; HERE YOU CAN SPEAK YOUR MIND AND BE YOURSELF. OPEN YOUR HEART AND LET MOTHER EARTH'S LOVE FILL YOU WITH HAPPINESS AND JOY.'

When you feel rejuvenated, open your eyes and repeat this incantation:

☆

'I AM CONNECTED TO THE ETERNAL SPIRIT OF LIGHT.'

Lost and found

YOU WILL NEED TO GATHER:

- *a large piece of paper or cardboard*
- *pen or pencil*
- *a piece of amber*

✮ On the night of a full moon draw a good-sized circle onto a large piece of paper or cardboard and place it on the floor near the last place you recalled seeing your lost item. Hold a piece of amber in your hand and stand in the centre of your circle. Relax your mind and body as you turn slowly in a clockwise direction, repeating this incantation:

✮

'AMBER SPIRIT OF THE LOST AND FOUND, SHOW ME THE WAY.'

As you turn you may feel the amber getting warmer at different points. This will give you a hint as to where you might find the lost article.

Fly me to the moon

YOU WILL NEED TO GATHER:

- *a feather*
- *a small bell*

☆ Dreams of flying can be a beautiful connection with the spirit and can really unite your creative and intuitive energy. Before you go to sleep at night, place a feather and a small bell near your bed and sit in a comfortable position as you breathe calmly and deeply for a few moments. Pick up the bell and ring it three times as you repeat this incantation:

Then place the feather under your pillow each night.

'AS I RING, MY HEART SINGS
AND THROUGH MY DREAMS
I SHALL FLY.'

Home sweet home

YOU WILL NEED
TO GATHER:

- *a cat's eye crystal*
- *a piece of rose quartz*
- *some spring water*
- *a clean white cloth*
- *a glass jar*

☆ To bring good vibes into the home, go to a crystal shop and purchase a small 'cat's eye' crystal and a rose quartz. On the night of a new moon, wash the cat's eye and quartz in spring water and, after drying it with a clean white cloth, walk through your home with both stones, repeating these words:

'MAGICA,
MISTICO,
BRING FORTH
YOUR CIRCLE
OF POWER
TO PROTECT
MY HOME
AND HEARTH.'

Then put the cat's eye in a glass jar somewhere in your home and keep the quartz crystal in your pocket.

Family trouble

☆ To help you grow some friendly vibrations with troublesome family members, rise early on a sunny Sunday morning and go outside and sit cross-legged next to a tree. Stay there for about twenty minutes. As you sit on the ground, straighten your back and spine and centre yourself as you feel the weight of your body connecting with the earth, almost as if you had roots. At the same time, feel the top of your head becoming light and lifting towards the sky as you raise your arms in the air and repeat this incantation:

When you feel empowered enough, stand up and take a twig from the tree. Keep the twig near your front door.

'O DELIA, GODDESS OF THE HARVEST, GRANT ME THE STRENGTH TO GROW CLOSE TO MY FAMILY. LET THEM SEE MY TRUE HEART.'

Doggy patrol

☆ Is your pooch a wanderer? If so, you could draw in some protective energy by making a special charm for it to wear. The colour brown is good for animals as it soothes

58

their auras, so buy your dog a brown collar, preferably made of leather, and as you place it around his neck say:

☆

'SANTA
FRANCESCO,
PROTECT THIS
ANIMAL
FROM HARM.'

Then, before you hook his identification tag to the collar, hold the tag in your hand and focus your mind on seeing a warm, happy glow around him as you repeat this incantation:

☆

'WHILE YOU
WEAR THIS
CHARM
MAY YOU
NEVER STRAY FAR
FROM HOME.'

Psychic power

☆ Even scientists are now accepting the fact that we are all surrounded by energy waves. Our bodies and minds are actually made up of energy, so it does stand to reason that, with enough practice, we could all become more intuitive and psychic beings. It only takes a few minutes a day to practise this spell but it works like a charm.

Sit quietly alone, relaxing your mind and body completely by listening to the sound of your breathing and heartbeat. Then, with your fingertips, lightly touch the centre of your forehead between your eyes and imagine that there is an opening there which is emitting a shaft of white light. Repeat these words:

'AS SWIFT AS MERCURY,
MY THOUGHTS ARE AS STRONG
AS THE RAYS OF SUNLIGHT.
MY VISION IS CLEAR
AND I HAVE SECOND SIGHT.'

Butterflies are free

☆ To help attract beautiful butterflies to your garden, find an area which receives lots of light and air. An open space near a window is fine if you don't have a back yard. On a Sunday morning, gather together some pots filled with sweet-smelling and brightly coloured flowers (try carnations, geraniums and honeysuckle) and place them around you in a circle. Sit in a comfortable position inside the circle and repeat this incantation:

If you have a garden, plant the flowers in your back yard. If you live in an apartment, just keep the pots on your balcony.

'CALANTHA, CHLOE,
I CALL ON THE PRECIOUS ALDORA.
FILL THE AIR WITH GENTLE WINGS.'

Don't worry, be happy

YOU WILL NEED
TO GATHER:

- *primrose oil*
- *a little spring water*
- *a pinch of thyme*
- *a bowl and a wooden spoon*
- *some light-coloured clothing*

☆ Niggling worries can keep you from enjoying your life to the full. Perform this magic ritual and bring back the happiness you deserve.

On the night of a new moon, mix together in a bowl seven drops of primrose oil (available from health food stores), five tablespoons of spring water and a pinch of thyme. Stir with a wooden spoon and repeat this incantation:

'KEEPERS OF ☆ THE SACRED FIRE, RISE UP AND FILL ME WITH STRENGTH OF THE PHOENIX.'

Then take a long shower and imagine that you are washing all of the negative energy of the past away. After patting yourself dry, dress in some light-coloured clothing and pour the magic mixture down the drain as you say:

'HERE FLOWS ALL MY PAIN, ☆ TO BE REPLACED BY SUNSHINE AGAIN.'

Begin again

☆ We can all feel stuck in a rut sometimes, but this spell with help you start afresh.

On the evening of a new moon, gather together one length of yellow ribbon, one length of green ribbon and one length of white ribbon, each approximately 30 cm (one foot) long. Sit down and braid the pieces of ribbon together while you repeat this incantation:

Tie up the ends of the braided ribbon and hold it whenever you feel stressed.

'OH SHIMMERING RIBBON,
GOLD, GREEN AND WHITE,
WEAVE YOUR MAGIC SPELL TONIGHT.
HELP ME FEEL MY SOUL WITHIN,
SO MY WONDERFUL NEW LIFE
CAN NOW BEGIN.'

I will survive

✧ If you observe the cycles of nature you'll notice that there is a time for stillness and hibernation, followed by a period of rebirth and action.

This continuous pattern is part of the normal ebb and flow of life, and the more you can listen to your instincts, the better will you understand that each phase is really a positive experience.

To help you feel empowered and balanced, take a shower and dress in a green shirt or dress. Let go of any negative thoughts and look up to the sky as you repeat this incantation:

☆

'FROM DARK TO LIGHT MOVES
THE GODDESS MOON, FROM DAY
TO NIGHT AND BACK AGAIN.
CYCLES OF LIFE MOVING ME FORWARD
THROUGH MY TRUE DESTINY.'

Don't
disturb

YOU WILL NEED
TO GATHER:

- *a small magnet*
- *a bowl*
- *some mineral water*

☆ Why put up with
noisy neighbours when
you can bring back
your privacy with a
wave of your wand?

Begin your spell by finding a small magnet and leaving it in a bowl of mineral water for one night in a place near a window. In the morning, take out the magnet and hold it in your hand as you walk resolutely to your front door, saying these magic words out loud:

Keep the magnet in your pocket and wash your door handles with the leftover mineral water.

'BEGONE! LET DISTURBANCE CEASE!
BLESSED BE THE CELESTIAL SPIRIT
WHO BRINGS PEACE.'

Peacemaker

☆ If you wish to clear up an argument, cast this spell on the morning of a new moon.

YOU WILL NEED TO GATHER:

- *three pebbles*
- *some spring water*
- *a piece of orange cloth*
- *talcum powder*

Wash three pebbles in spring water and, after drying them with an orange cloth, sprinkle them with talcum powder as you repeat this incantation:

☆

'SMALLER, SMALLER, THOSE WORDS OF ANGER DISSOLVE LIKE CLOUDS IN THE WIND.'

Then pick up the stones one at a time. As you hold them in your hands concentrate on letting go of your hurt and stress and repeat these words:

☆

'WISHING RELATES TO THE END, AN ENEMY NOW IS A FRIEND.'

Finish the spell by throwing the stones into a pond or a river.

Hercules

YOU WILL NEED
TO GATHER:

- *a glass of lemonade*
- *fresh ginger*
- *a few mint leaves*

☆ Thoughts are
powerful rays of energy
that can materialise
whatever we are
sincerely focused on.
If you have a special

dream, help that wish come true with the power of Hercules.

Blend together a glass of lemonade with a few shavings of fresh ginger and a pinch of mint. Take a few sips and think about your wish as you try to feel your life force expanding, then say aloud:

'HERCULES, FILL THIS ENCHANTED BREW, AND ALLOW MY GREATNESS TO COME THROUGH.'

75

Money
and
Success

WINNING WAYS

Wealthy and wise

YOU WILL NEED
TO GATHER:

- *a silver candle*
- *a glass bowl*
- *notebook and pen*
- *two quartz crystals*
- *juniper essence*
- *frankincense essence*

☆ What does prosperity and wealth mean to you? Is it living comfortably, sharing fun and a few luxuries with close friends and family – or do you dream of vast riches and world fame?

Whatever your aspirations are, the first step in this spell is to define and focus on your wishes by writing them down in your notebook as a mission statement. Read each of your ambitions through carefully, then place the notebook on a table between the two crystals. Light the candle, and as you drip a little of the juniper and frankincense

essences into the bowl repeat this incantation:

'ARTEMIS, DARIUS,
CALL ABUNDANCE
MY WAY.
MY DREAMS SHALL
COME TRUE.
SO MOTE IT BE.'

Blow out the candle after twenty minutes, then sprinkle the mixed essence around your home or office. Keep the notebook and the crystals near your bed.

Car charmer

☆ If you wish to get a good price for your car, the day before you advertise it for sale, perform this washing ritual.

Mix in a teaspoon of lemon juice to a bucket of sudsy water. Walk around the car clockwise once and splash a little of the water onto the front hood as you say the brand name of the car out loud three times, and then repeat this incantation:

☆

'I PURIFY YOU
WITH THIS
WATER.'

Wash the car completely and then, with the final polishing, say:

☆

'I POLISH YOU
WITH
SUCCESS.'

81

Get that job

YOU WILL NEED
TO GATHER:

- *lavender*
- *nutmeg*
- *a few bay leaves*
- *a piece of cheesecloth*
- *a length of blue ribbon*

☆ If you're looking
for new employment,
the best time to cast
this spell will be at
either 9 am or 9 pm.

Look through your local newspaper in the job section and circle the ads that appeal to you. Lay the paper on a table and sprinkle some lavender, nutmeg and a few bay leaves over the top as you repeat this incantation:

Then tip the same mixture onto a piece of cheesecloth and tie up the ends with blue ribbon so as to make a small pouch. When you go for a job interview, carry the magic pouch with you in your pocket.

'BY THE POWER OF JUPITER,
WITH THE LUCK OF ZEUS,
GRANT ME THE JOB
THAT WILL BRING SUCCESS.'

Tiger by the tail

YOU WILL NEED TO GATHER:

- *tiger balm (available from health food stores)*
- *ginger*
- *fresh coriander*
- *a glass bowl*
- *a piece of red paper and a pen*
- *a length of gold string*
- *a box*

☆ In Asian culture, tigers are considered to have mystical qualities of vigour and potency. If your cash flow is slowing down, this spell will help you channel some of that feline strength to top up your bank balance.

On a Wednesday evening at 8 pm, mix together in a glass bowl a small quantity of tiger balm with some grated ginger and coriander. Write down the amount of money you need (be specific or you will scatter the spell's energy) onto a piece of red paper, then wipe the magic mixture over the paper and say:

'WITH THE STAMINA OF THE TIGER, WITH THE KNOWLEDGE OF THE OLD ONES, I WALK THE ROAD TO PROSPERITY.'

✫

Roll the paper into a ball, tie it up with some gold string and keep it in a box near your money documents.

I'm a genius

☆ Whether you are studying for an exam or wanting to expand your mind power, this spell with help you tap into the infinite wisdom of the Universe.

YOU WILL NEED TO GATHER:

● *dried cloves*
● *fresh mint leaves*
● *a glass bowl*

Half an hour before your studying session, take a shower and dress in some clean, comfortable clothes. Stand near an open window. Sprinkle some cloves in a clockwise direction around you. Then step inside the circle and stand with your arms outstretched while you repeat this incantation:

After you have taken three deep breaths, rub some mint leaves in your hands and keep the mint and the cloves in a glass bowl near your study table.

'THANK YOU, O UNIVERSE,
FOR THIS BODY AND MIND.
AS I BREATHE IN THE COSMIC FORCES
I SHALL FOCUS WITH CONFIDENCE
AND KNOWLEDGE.'

Bon voyage

YOU WILL NEED
TO GATHER:

- *ginger*
- *seaweed*

☆ When you want to go on a fabulous holiday, cast this charm on a Sunday morning.

Stand near a stretch of water (a river, lake or the ocean) while holding the root of a ginger and some seaweed in your hand. Focus your mind on the type of trip you would like and then gaze into the water as you repeat this incantation:

Throw the ginger and the seaweed into the water and then close your eyes and imagine you are already on your holiday having a great time.

'BY THE POWER OF NEPTUNE,
BY THE GODS OF THE SEA,
GRANT ME GOOD TRAVELLING
AND SO SHALL IT BE.'

Legal eagle

YOU WILL NEED TO GATHER:

- ◗ *dandelion tea leaves*
- ◗ *a lemon*
- ◗ *a glass jar with a lid*
- ◗ *a glass of spring water*
- ◗ *a white cloth*

☆ If you have legal problems or are facing a court case, cast this spell on a Thursday morning or evening at 7 o'clock.

Mix together a teaspoon of dandelion tea and a teaspoon of

lemon juice and keep the mixture in a glass jar with a lid. In the weeks leading up to your court appearance, pour one drop of the liquid into a glass of spring water, light a blue candle and repeat this incantation:

Sprinkle a little of the magic water onto a white cloth and wipe down your doors and window sills with the cloth once a week until the case is heard. For extra power, wear something blue on the day of your court appearance.

'I WEAVE THIS SPELL
WITH JUSTICE AND MIGHT,
THAT ALL BE DONE
FOR THE GOOD AND RIGHT.'

Land sale

YOU WILL NEED
TO GATHER:

● *fresh or dried rosemary,
basil and marjoram*

● *a potted rosemary plant*

☆ Call on the
Nature spirits to help
you sell your block of
land. On the day of a
waxing moon (moving
from new to full) go
to the land and walk
around the centre of it

three times carrying a fresh or dried bunch of herbs. Imagine that a peaceful golden light is flowing over the land and repeat this incantation:

Finish the spell by planting some rosemary on the block of land.

'MERRY MERRY MEET,
ANCESTORS ALL BLESS THIS EARTH
SO I MAY PASS IT ON.'

Cheapskate charm

☆ It can be so upsetting to be owed money by a cheapskate. To help you get your money back, cast this spell on a Monday evening, or, for extra power, on a night of a full moon.

Take a nail file and carve the amount you are owed into the side of a purple candle. Then sprinkle some salt around it in a clockwise direction and light the candle for around twenty minutes.

As you sit comfortably nearby, concentrate on visualising the person owing you the money. Imagine you are speaking directly to them as you repeat this incantation:

Repeat this spell once a week, until the candle is completely melted down. Keep the remaining wax near your money documents.

'WHILE MONEY IS OWED TO
THOSE WHO WAIT,
BILLS PILE UP AND CONFUSION REIGNS.
YOUR CONSCIENCE SHALL PRICK
WHEN I REPEAT THIS PLEA,
ALLOW WHAT IS MINE TO
RETURN TO ME.'

Office harmony

YOU WILL NEED
TO GATHER:

- *a white feather*
- *one white candle*
- *two purple candles*
- *vanilla essence*

☆ Tired of
tiresome office politics
and grumpy bosses?
To clean out any
unharmonious energy,
try this spell.

Find a white feather and place it near one white and two purple candles on a table. Think about each of your workmates as you light the three candles and repeat these words:

☆

'LIGHTER THAT LIGHT, SOFTER THAN A FEATHER, PROBLEMS FLOAT AWAY.'

Sprinkle a few drops of vanilla essence over the feather and then wave it near the candles (not too close to the flame) as you repeat the incantation three times. When you blow out the candles, say:

☆

'AND SO IT WILL COME TO PASS.'

Take the feather to work with you in your pocket or briefcase.

Cast a rune

☆ The modern Runes have been adapted from ancient Nordic and Druid symbols. As well as divining the future, they can be used to manifest a positive outcome with a spell.

The next time you cast your Runes, ask your question and then throw the stones until they give you a favourable answer. Concentrate on seeing this positive outcome and then light a white candle and repeat these words:

Leave the stones untouched for at least an hour.

'FROM CAILLAN TO CALDER
BY ATLANTIS,
BEHOLD THE LIGHT OF TRUTH.'

Faerie luck

YOU WILL NEED
TO GATHER:

- *straw*
- *ferns*
- *ivy*
- *a length of green wool*
- *dried wild flowers*
- *spring water*
- *rosehip tea*

☆ You can ask the Faeries to help anoint your home and business with good fortune and prosperity.

Make a magic wreath by gathering together some straw, ferns and ivy and weave them all up in circle with a piece of green wool. Add some dried wild flowers for decoration, then spray the wreath with a fine mist of spring water that has been mixed with a little rosehip tea.

Next, walk around each room in your home or office once in a clockwise direction while holding the magic wreath. Finally, hang the wreath near your front door as you repeat this incantation:

'COME IN FROM THE MIST
OF SILVERY DEW,
COME GATHER, DANCE AND PLAY,
PIXIES, ELVES AND FAERIES ALL.
LAUGHTER RINGS LIKE
TINKLING BELLS.'

Money money money

YOU WILL NEED
TO GATHER:

- *a piece of pyrite ('fool's gold')*
- *a green candle*
- *three coins*
- *a piece of green cloth*

☆ To help attract money towards you, cast this spell on the night of a full or waxing moon.

Purchase a small piece of pyrite from a crystal shop. Light a green candle and place the pyrite on a table with three coins nearby. Pick up the coins in your hands and try to feel a warm, soothing energy around you as you say:

Then throw the coins onto the table as you focus your thoughts on the amount of money you desire. Wrap up the pyrite and coins in a green cloth, and as you blow out the candle say:

'AND SO SHALL IT BE.'

'MAY ALL THAT I GIVE AND ALL THAT I RECEIVE RETURN THREEFOLD TO THE WORLD AND THREEFOLD TO ME.'

Creative circle

✫ To get your creative juices flowing, cast a Magic circle around you by standing in a quiet space in your home. As you hold your arms in the air, turn to the north as you say:

✫

'SPIRIT OF THE NORTH
GRANT ME WISDOM
AND TOLERANCE.'

Then turn to the south
as you say:

☆

'SOUTHERN SKY,
PURIFY
MY THOUGHT.'

Then finish by
turning to the west
and saying:

☆

'WESTERN
WATERS,
GRANT ME
FEELING AND
EMOTION.'

As you turn to the
east say:

☆

'EASTERN DAWN,
GRANT ME
NEW IDEAS.'

Wish on a star

YOU WILL NEED
TO GATHER:

- *light-coloured clothing*
- *three sticks of sandlewood incense*
- *pen and white paper*

☆ Why wait for a falling star to make your special wish? You can create your own lucky star to help fulfil your hopes and dreams.

106

On a Thursday evening, dress in some clean, light-coloured clothing and light three sticks of sandalwood incense. Draw a five-pointed star onto a piece of white paper and stick it onto the inside of your front door. Stand in the middle of your home as you imagine that all your worries are streaming away from you like a river and in its place flows happiness and good health. Then place your right hand onto the lucky star and repeat this incantation:

'STELLA ANISE, SACRED STAR OF ENCHANTMENT, GLOW WITH THE VISION OF HAPPINESS AND FORTUNE FOR ALL OF US TO SHARE.'

The frog prince

✫ When an ex-husband or partner is acting like a complete toad, try this spell to help turn them back into Prince Charming.

Find a medium-sized square of calico or muslin and sew up the sides with green cotton to make a pouch. Leave one side open.

Pour a few teaspoons of sand into the pouch while focusing on letting go of all your stress and resentment.

Then sprinkle in some violet petals and a handful of chicken feathers (stuffing from an old feather pillow will do fine). Tie up the end of the pouch with a green ribbon and write the frog prince's full name on the bag.

Then place the bag on top of a small mirror and say:

'WHEN YOU'RE BEING A TOAD, O BLESSED BE; IN A MIRROR'S GAZE YOUR REAL SELF YOU'LL SEE. SO BE IT AND LET IT BE.'

Finally, sprinkle some vanilla essence over the top of everything, wrap it in white paper, and throw it in the bin.

Naughty Spells

Spells

SORCERY FOR STRESS

Warrior Queen

✫ Empower yourself with the all-encompassing energy of the 'Triple Goddess' by casting this spell during a new or waxing moon (when the moon is moving from new to full).

Take a relaxing bath or shower and anoint your body with your favorite floral oils and perfumes.

Remain undressed and go to your bedroom, where you light a stick of geranium or rose incense and a mauve candle. Sit in a comfortable position and breathe in the aroma of the incense as you concentrate on how all the different aspects of yourself help balance your life. Then say aloud:

'I AM THE WARRIOR QUEEN
FULL OF STRENGTH AND
DEFENDING MY RIGHTS.
I AM THE YOUNG MAIDEN, GENTLE
AND NURTURING.
I AM THE MYSTIC GODDESS, SPIRITUALLY
WISE, FEMININE AND FREE.
I AM ALL ASPECTS OF WOMAN,
ALL IN PERFECT HARMONY.'

Road rage balm

YOU WILL NEED TO GATHER:

● *two tablespoons of Vaseline (petroleum jelly)*

● *two drops of basil essential oil*

● *three drops of sandalwood essential oil*

● *two drops of bergamot essential oil*

● *a teaspoon of finely chopped carnation petals*

☆ You've been sitting in traffic for hours. You're late for work, and someone starts screaming at you over a parking space.

No hassle, just dab on a little Road Rage Balm.

The best time to mix up a batch of Road Rage Balm is on a Friday, preferably during a full or new moon. Mix the ingredients well in a glass bowl while you charge the formula with protective magic by saying:

⭐

'I CHARGE YOU
BY THE SUN
AND MOON
TO PROTECT
AND DRIVE OFF
NEGATIVITY.
SPREAD
SOOTHING CALM
WHERE YOU
ARE RUBBED;
IT SHALL BE DONE,
O BLESSED BE.'

Then spoon the mixture into a small clean jar and firmly screw the lid on. Keep the jar in your car or purse and dab a small amount of the balm behind your ears whenever needed.

Holy smoke

☆ If you've been having trouble giving up cigarettes, cast this spell on the day of the moon, Monday. Gather together a deflated party balloon and a sprig of mint.

Place them on a flat surface or a table in front of you. Meditate for a few minutes while you release any tension from your mind and body.

Then hold the mint in your hand and breathe in the aroma. As you breathe deeply and evenly, repeat this incantation:

'LET ALL
IMPURITIES BE
CAST FROM ME
WITH THIS
CLEANSING
BREATH.'

Next, blow air into the party balloon until it is full and tie a knot in the end. Then open a window or go outside and throw the balloon up in the air as you say:

'SO WILL IT BE.'

Keep a fresh spring of mint with you always and whenever you feel a craving coming on, breathe in its aroma and repeat the incantation.

Fatal attraction

☆ If a *femme fatale* is trying to steal your lover, or an ex-partner is harassing you, you could sour their chances by performing this ancient spell.

Saturday is one of the best days for banishing or protection enchantments, so find a time in the day that suits you. Gather a lemon and a teaspoon of sea salt and place them on a table.

Sit nearby while you write the person's name on a piece of paper backwards nine times with all the letters joining into a long line. Next, put the paper into a glass bowl, sprinkle it with salt, then squeeze juice from the lemon over the top while saying:

'BITTER AND TART, RIGHT FROM THE START, GO ELSEWHERE TO FEATHER YOUR NEST;

BY THE CALL OF THE CROW ON RAVEN'S NIGHT, LEAVE US BE! GO WALK IN THE LIGHT! IT SHALL BE SO, AND IT WILL BE RIGHT.'

Leave the paper soaking overnight in the magic mixture. Then dig a hole in the ground near your home, pour everything in and cover with earth.

Witch's broomstick

☆ We're all familiar with the image of a witch flying her broomstick, usually wearing a pointed hat. This image has become a cartoonish stereotype, but the broom is actually an important tool in Magick. It not only cleans the floor of many a suburban goddess's temple, but it also sweeps out bad vibes and with the right incantation, helps to create an enchanted circle.

To begin, take a simple straw broom with a wooden handle and tie one gold and one green ribbon onto the handle while saying these words:

'MY HOME IS MY TEMPLE AND THIS BROOM IS MY LUCKY CHARM.'

Then walk around each room of your home holding the broom. Imagine that you are sweeping away unwanted energy and clearing the way for the new. Finish by standing in your living room and sweep around yourself in a clockwise direction as you say:

'HERE NOW I CREATE THE CIRCLE OF THE MYSTIC GODDESS. BRUSH GOOD FORTUNE AND LUCK OUR WAY. O BLESSED BE.'

Busybody brew

☆ To diminish the power of gossip and lies, cast this spell on a Sunday morning or evening.

Gather together a loaf of white bread, a piece of paper, a pencil and some chilli powder.

On the piece of paper, write down all the lies and rumours you've heard and then slice a hole in the loaf of bread and stuff the paper inside. Sprinkle a little chilli powder over the top as you say these magic words:

Then wrap the bread up in newspaper and throw it all away in the garbage bin.

'CLEAN AND CLEAR BECOME THE WORDS
THAT ARE SPOKEN AS GOSSIP AND LIES.
AS THIS LOAF BEGINS TO STALE AND DRY
FAR AWAY DOES SLANDER FLY.'

Copycat

☆ Don't you just hate it when someone copies everything you do? They might copy how you dress or wear your hair, or even steal your original ideas or work.

To protect your individual style and ideas, write the person's name on a piece of paper, or hold a photograph of the copycat as you meditate for a few minutes. Imagine that a ring of light is encircling you both like a hula hoop. Visualise the power of your words as an electrical force that sends karmic energy along the hoop of light. Then repeat this incantation:

'AS ARTISTRY IS USED IN VAIN,
AS INVENTIVENESS IS LOST AGAIN,
AS ORIGINALITY IS ONCE MORE
DENIED, AS STEALING THE VISION
IS NOW TRIED, SO LET IMITATION
BE EXPOSED TO THE LIGHT.'

★ Most magic rituals use tools like candles, aromatic incenses, herbs and spices. Each herb, colour and scent has its own special vibration which will enhance the individual power of your spell.

CANDLE MAGIC

Red – passionate love, vitality and strength
Orange – health, creativity and energy
Green – luck, prosperity and healing
Yellow – focus, awareness and happiness
Blue – success, peace and tranquillity
Purple – spirituality, psychic ability and mysticism
Pink – friendship, love and femininity
White – truth, purity and meditation
Brown – animal magic, earth and environment
Gold – the sun, wealth and royalty
Silver – the moon, prosperity and enchantment

HERBS AND INCENSE

Basil – wealth, love and success

Cinnamon – luck, passion and prosperity

Clove – memory, insight and attraction

Eucalyptus – healing, cleansing and uplifting

Frankincense – high magic and purification

Gardenia – arousing, passionate, lust

Garlic – banishing and protection

Jasmine – spiritual love and happiness

Juniper – safety, affection and friendship

Lavender – attraction, sexuality and femininity

Mint – cleansing, uplifting, clear sight

Nutmeg – money, attraction, clairvoyance

Rose – love, passion and ambrosia

Rosemary – healing, good fortune and high magic

Sandalwood – meditation, tranquillity, mental ability

Sage – purification, prosperity and health

Thyme – cleansing, renewing, luck

Vanilla – purity, feminine attraction, affection

MOON POWER

Full moon – for casting spells of love and high magic
New moon – to begin a brand new relationship or job
Waxing or growing moon – to attract growth,
prosperity and commitment
Waning or diminishing moon – to finish a relationship
or to banish negative energy

DAYS OF ENCHANTMENT

Sunday – divine power, for casting spells
of healing and tranquillity
Monday – beginnings, mysticism, employment
Tuesday – courage, strength, passion
Wednesday – communications, predictions, learning
Thursday – legal matters, luck, expansion
Friday – love, pleasure, art, music
Saturday – departure, finalisation, resolution